Dress Up
Kate

Illustrated by
Georgie Fearns

Edited by
Jen Wainwright

Designed by Zoe Quayle

First published in Great Britain in 2012 by Buster Books, an imprint of
Michael O'Mara Books Limited, 9 Lion Yard, Tremadoc Road, London SW4 7NQ

www.busterbooks.co.uk

Copyright © 2012 Buster Books

ISBN: 978-1-78055-026-8

4 6 8 10 9 7 5 3

This book was printed in July 2012 by Ruho Corporation Sdn. Bhd.,
334 Sungai Puyu, 13020 Butterworth, Penang, Malaysia.

Buster Books

Contents

It's Time To Dress Up Kate

Ever since Kate Middleton married Prince William and became the Duchess of Cambridge, she has been admired for her beauty and her sophisticated sense of style. From the world's most talked-about wedding dress, to her favourite designers and her choice of accessories – everyone wants to know what Kate will be wearing next.

Now you have the chance to decide on Kate's royal wardrobe. You can be Kate's stylist in Hollywood, at a gala dinner, on her romantic honeymoon and at many other glamorous events. Use the fantastic stickers to dress up Kate and complete the scenes for each colourful occasion shown in this book.

There are even some extra stickers that you can use to decorate stuff.

A Garden Party

Kate is at the Queen's garden party in the grounds of Buckingham Palace. Everyone is dressed in their finest clothes. At the party, the guests will nibble more than 20,000 slices of cake and sip 27,000 cups of tea. Dress up Kate and complete the summer scene.

5

Kate's Wedding Day

Kate marries her handsome prince, William, at Westminster Abbey, in London. She is wearing a beautiful wedding dress made of ivory and white silk, decorated with delicate lace embroidery in patterns of pretty flowers. Complete the wedding party.

A Royal Honeymoon

After the excitement of their wedding day, Kate and William
jet off to the Seychelles – a tropical island paradise.
With its white sand, hot sun, palm trees and clear blue ocean,
it is the perfect place for the newlyweds to relax and
enjoy themselves. Dress the happy couple for
a chilled-out day at the beach.

A Gala Dinner

Kate and Prince William like to show their support for lots of charities. Tonight, they are at a glamorous gala dinner in London, which will raise money for an international children's charity. Dress up Kate in a stunning pale pink dress with sparkling sequins. Later, William will make a speech, then some famous bands will take to the stage.

11

At Balmoral

Kate, her in-laws, Prince Charles and Camilla, and the Queen, are visiting the castle of Balmoral in Scotland. Dress them for a walk in the beautiful forests and valleys.

HOLLYWOOD

Hooray For Hollywood!

Tom Hanks is with William and Kate at an awards ceremony in LA. Dress them for the red carpet, then dress Nicole Kidman and Jennifer Lopez, too.

14

A Lifeboat Launch

Kate helps to launch a lifeboat in Anglesey, Wales, by pouring champagne over it. Dress up Kate for the windy weather in a warm but stylish winter coat.

Joyous Jubilee

The Queen celebrates her Diamond Jubilee, marking 60 years of her reign. Neighbours and friends gather for street parties, with cakes and delicious food. Kate and the Queen are visiting this street. Dress up Kate smartly for the occasion, and finish off Her Majesty's outfit, too.

19

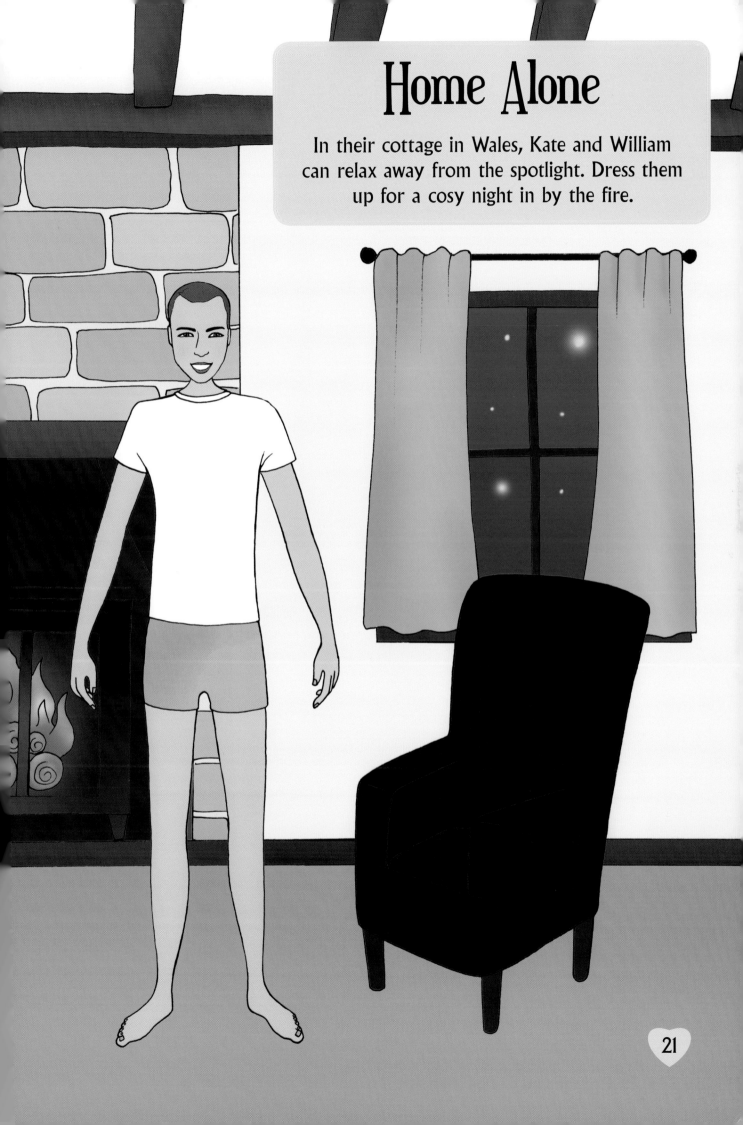

Home Alone

In their cottage in Wales, Kate and William can relax away from the spotlight. Dress them up for a cosy night in by the fire.

21

Flying Away

Kate and William are visiting Canada and the USA.
A crowd wishes them well on their journey home.
Dress up the couple for this stylish state visit.

It's A Wrap

Add pretty shapes and patterns to Kate's favourite wrap dress.

24

glamorous guest

pitchers of punch

jacket

Kate's bag

beautiful butterflies

A Garden Party
pages 4 – 5

dainty cucumber sandwiches

regal hat
and coat

tea service

crowning glory

Kate's bouquet

sash for bridesmaid's dress

bridesmaids' bouquets and hair garlands

Kate's veil

Kate's Wedding Day
pages 6 – 7

Union Jacks

Wills' sash and medals

love is in the air!

star quality!

Wills' hat

belt tasse

Harry's hat

Kate's tiara

roses for romance

sun vizor

swooping gulls

swimming turtle

coconut cocktails

flower garland

lobster salad

speedboat

A Royal Honeymoon
pages 8 – 9

seashells, seashells on the seashore

yacht ahoy!

his and hers shades

diving dolphins

deckchair

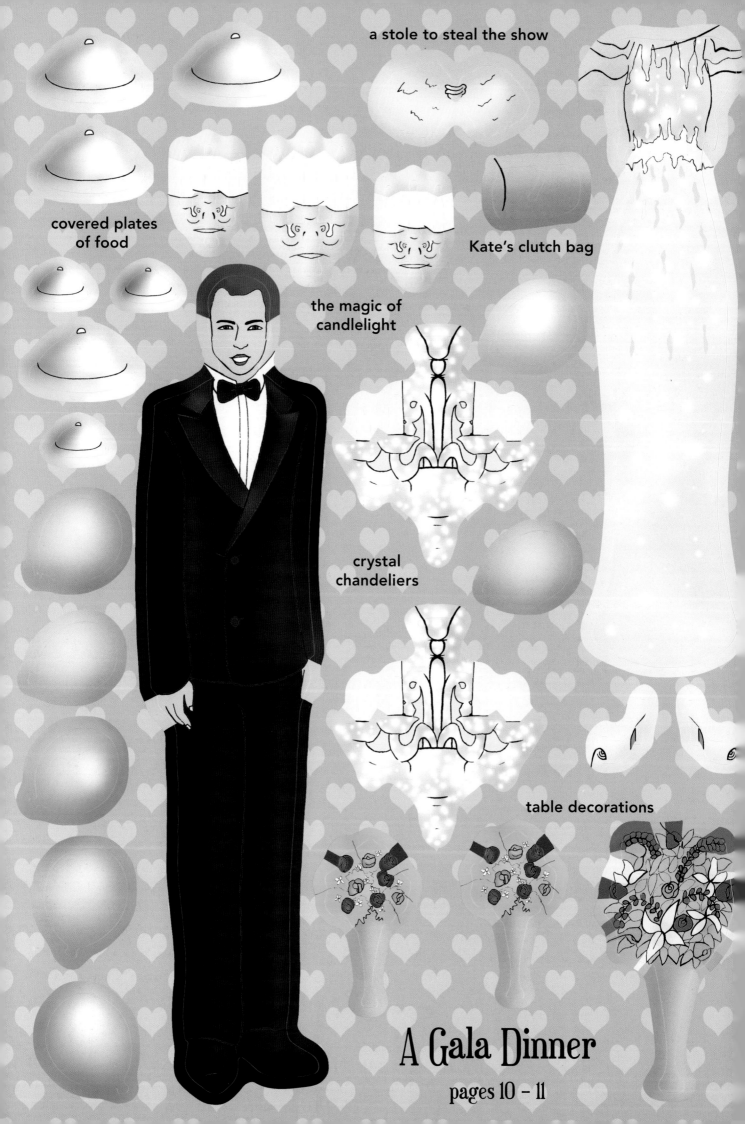

a stole to steal the show

covered plates
of food

Kate's clutch bag

the magic of
candlelight

crystal
chandeliers

table decorations

A Gala Dinner
pages 10 – 11

At Balmoral
pages 12 -13

a coat for Charles

scarf

the Queen's headscarf

gloves fit for the Queen

the Queen's walking stick

a coat for Charles' dog

picnic basket

caps

corgis

grouse are fair game

umbrella

boots for Camilla

royal rocks

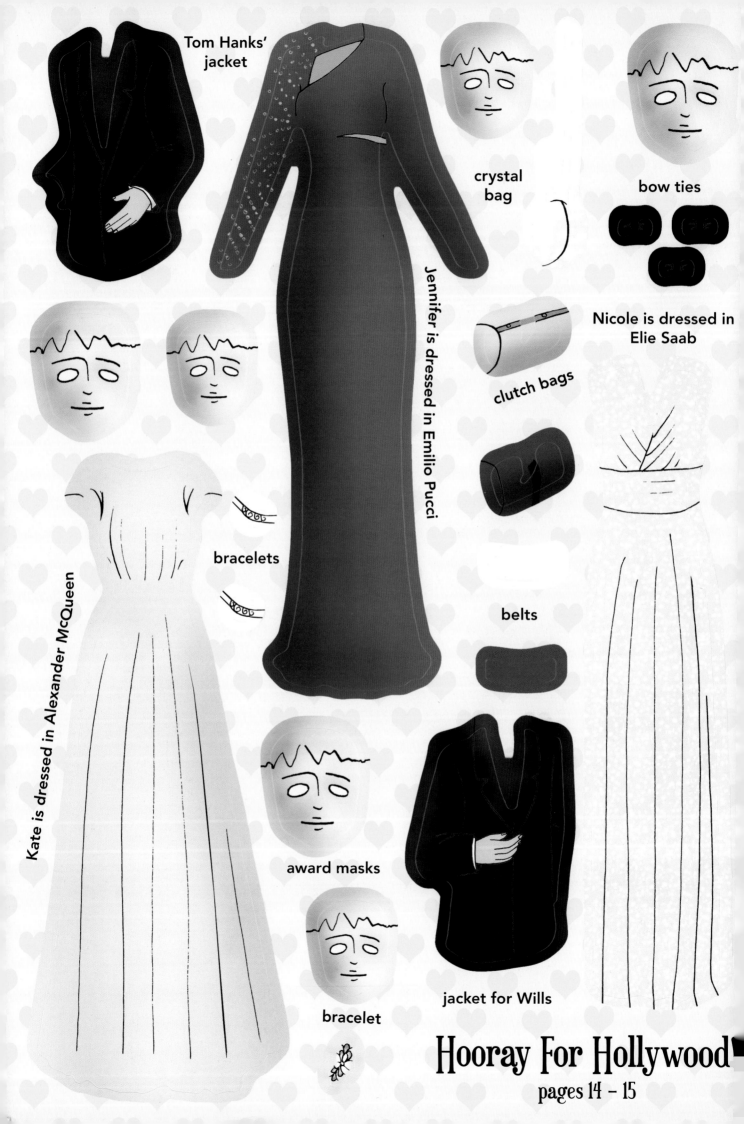

Tom Hanks' jacket

crystal bag

bow ties

Nicole is dressed in Elie Saab

Jennifer is dressed in Emilio Pucci

clutch bags

bracelets

belts

Kate is dressed in Alexander McQueen

award masks

jacket for Wills

bracelet

Hooray For Hollywood
pages 14 – 15

life jacket for the boatman

medal

microphone

Champagne to christen the boat

seagulls

ship's cat

A Lifeboat Launch
pages 16 – 17

leggings

Kate's hat and scarf

Wills' tie

Kate's gloves

the sun shone

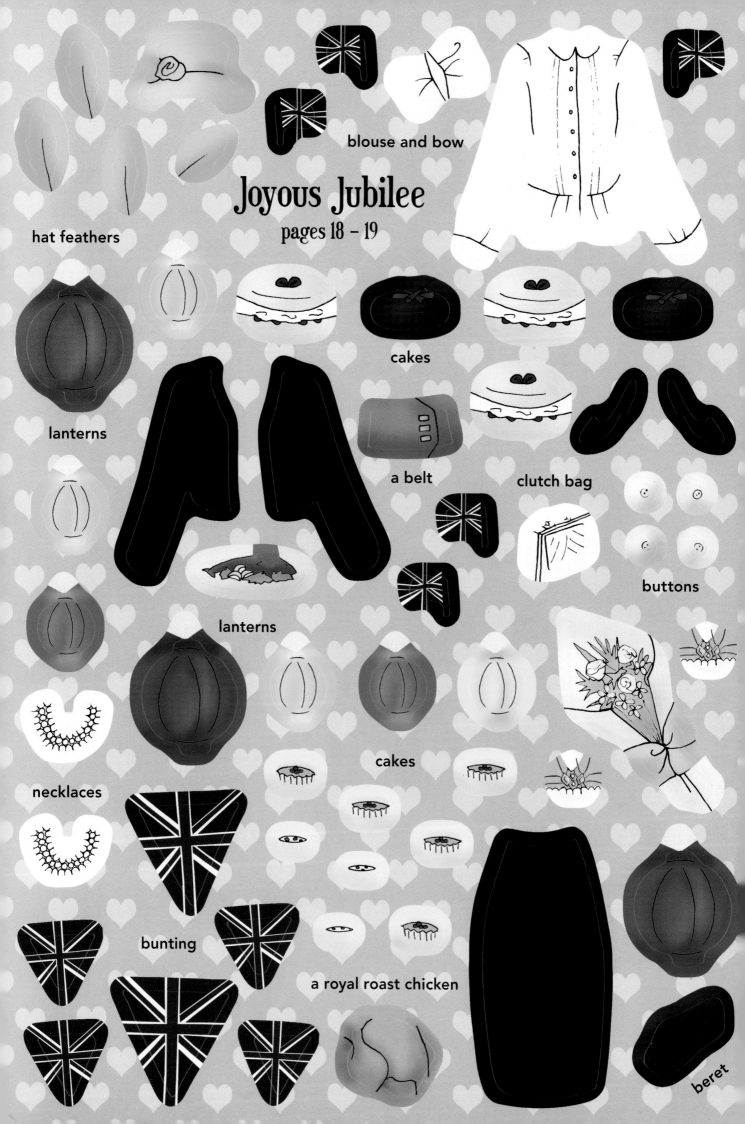

hat feathers

blouse and bow

Joyous Jubilee
pages 18 – 19

cakes

lanterns

a belt

clutch bag

buttons

lanterns

cakes

necklaces

bunting

a royal roast chicken

beret

royal
bust

lamp

his pjs

Home Alone
pages 20 – 21

her pjs

cat bowl

mugs of cocoa

cosy
slippers

Flying Away

bangle

pages 22 – 23

wills   Kate

Kate's cape

clutch bag

Wills' tie
and jacket

windows

hat

It's A Wrap

page 24